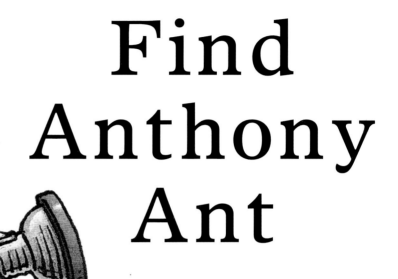

Find
Anthony
Ant

This edition first published in Great Britain in 2006
Reprinted twice in 2007
by Boxer Books Limited.
www.boxerbooks.com

First published in Great Britain in 1993
by Orion Children's Books, under the title
Amazing Anthony Ant.

ISBN 13: 978-1-905417-47-6

Printed in China

For Ann,
David and Nicola

Are you an amazing Anthony Ant
finder? If so, can you find the odd
one out among all the Anthony Ants
on the endpapers of this book?

Find Anthony Ant

Lorna and Graham Philpot

Start here

THE ANTHONY ANT WAY IN

THE ANTHONY ANT WAY OUT

Boxer Books

1

The ants came marching **one by one.** Anthony stopped...

WAY IN

BEETLE LANE

Grub Shop

PLUM TREE TRUNK ROAD

 or  or

To climb
a tree?

To watch
TV?

Because he's
hurt his knee?

Find Anthony Ant.

4

The ants came marching
four by four.
Anthony stopped...

LADYBIRD LANE

Anti Dorothy

ANT COLONY CLOSE

ANTI SHAFT

ANTI SHAFT

 or  or

To knock on
the door?

To ask
for more?

To sweep
the floor?

Find Anthony Ant.

ANTHRACITE VALE

Oliver's Restaur'ant

WEEVIL WAY

WORKER ANT WALK

5

The ants came marching
five by five.
Anthony stopped...

 or  or

To visit
a hive?

To jiggle
and jive?

To go for
a drive?

Find Anthony Ant.

Venus
Ant
trap

Underground
RAVE

SPRING
ROAD

Sub Aqua Ant

WORM
HOLE
WELL

6

The ants came marching
six by six.
Anthony stopped...

 or  or

To tickle the chicks?   To stack the bricks?   To perform magic tricks?

Find Anthony Ant.

ROTTEN WOOD WAY

BEECH TREE ROUTE

ANTI-THEATRE

1

2

3

7

The ants came marching
seven by seven.
Anthony stopped...

 or  or

To chat with
Kevin?

To hide in
a cavern?

To count
to eleven?

Find Anthony Ant.

EXPORT ANT LIFT

CAVERN RESTAUR'ANT

All Ants' Church

Infant School

8

The ants came marching
eight by eight.
Anthony stopped...

 or  or

To lick
his plate?

To look
for a gate?

To check
his weight?

Find Anthony Ant.

WALK

MAIN DRAIN STREET

9

The ants came marching
nine by nine.
Anthony stopped...

APPLE CORE COURT

UNDERWEAR WAY

Ants in Pants

APPLE TREE ROUTE

 or  or

To hang socks on the line?   To read a sign?   To shout, "That hat's mine"?

Find Anthony Ant.

10

The ants came marching
ten by ten.
Anthony stopped...

Antiques

RIBCAGE WALK

SKELETON WEST END

 or

To feed
the hen?

To write
with a pen?

To read
it again?

Find Anthony Ant.

Way In

Way Out

ALLANS' WAY

SKELETON · EAST · END

Did you find me?